To Mo,

An Island Road

A Souvenir of a Special Day,

By Philip Brady

Brady
January 5th 2000.

ACKNOWLEDGEMENTS

The author wishes to express his debt to those who helped in a material or inspirational way in making this work possible.

Preparation, Proof-Reading and Design:
Sarah Brady
Bernadette Brady

Published in Ireland by
Alesbury Books, Edenderry, Co. Offaly.
© Copyright – Philip Brady, 2007. All rights reserved.

Printed and bound by ColourBooks Ltd, Baldoyle, Dublin 13.

Some of these poems have previously appeared in:
The Irish Medical Journal, Treoir
The Balyna Annual, The Carmelite Contact &
The Edgeworth Papers

A catalogue for this book is available from the British Library.
ISBN No.   **978-0-9525027-5-3**

FOREWORD

An honour and privilege, unmerited by a simple practitioner of the word, to write an introduction to this, his 4th volume of Philip's poetry. My critical qualification - class-mate, a cousin, and friend!

Way back in St. Mel's, the weekly essay was a chore for most, a nail-biting exercise to somehow complete three foolscap pages with minimum unrelated participles and split-infinitives!! Even then Phil had a soft spot for "purple" passages and unusual Botanical words, always perfectly placed to the delight of our English pro Fr. Tommy O'Brien.

This edition speaks with authority. As he says, "the pen is a great friend." The G.P. from Edenderry is a specialist in his words and message, ranging from Celtic lament, biographical reflection, concern for the environment, the loneliness, alienation, and exploitation of non Irish Nationals, the acrid bitterness of child abuse, and the helplessness of his healing profession sometimes.

It is an incisive contemporary commentary – a *Magnum Opus* – hope you enjoy it!

Fr. Peter Brady

DEDICATION

For
Patricia
Sarah & Bernadette
Philip & Peter

Proof that
No man is an Island,
Entire of itself.

Donne

CONTENTS

A SERPENT

When Dionysus died
The whole town grew quiet
In a quick inhale of breath,
Afraid to let go
Or to release again.

The cortege was late,
And later still
The empty street would wait
And wait,
Until the young men came,
The soccer men,
The rugby men,
The Gaelic men,
The silent praying men,
The sometimes straying men,
The tattoo branded men,
All swaying,
In one long shuffling mile
After silent mile,
Classmates, soul mates
Boon mates, no mates;
The only sound
Was footfall
As if it trampled muffled snow.

On and on it wound,
A serpent weaving
Through the hollow town,
A casket in its carapace.
The young would walk
With floral frond,
And whisper worried talk,
For each one was a part
Of something come alive;
Their souls had unified,
The brave became the shaken,
With frailty undermined
Until they reached the waiting gates.

They filled the aisles,
The unfamiliar pew,
Where each was named
And some time grew,
The silent yard
That heaved and throbbed
And spilled with overflow
That sometimes sobbed,
Where each one would recall
The once familiar laugh or shout
Or call they one time knew.
All wondered if there could be some mistake,
For tragedy could not be entertained,
Nor could it be allowed to take
Someone
As indestructible
As you.

The town filled up again,
The house lights came
With blinked apology
As if to say
We must return to what we knew.
To north and south,
To east and west
The parts would drift away,
Reintegrate,
But fragments of their souls remained
That marched that day.
They knew that they had changed
Forever
With you.

FREEDOM

I saw the Taoiseach once
Out on the mountain,
Where the wild ling meets the bracken.
I was reading Synge
On a heather tuft,
The only student in that library.
The silence was broken.
A military step
On the military road
Intruded
On a symphony
Of silence, growing louder.
I peered between colluna frames
That one day would be purple.
There he was
The most powerful man in the Republic
On a mountain road
To Glean na Smól
Where the wild thrush sings
To polished car and polished leather,
The bodyguard in step,
Through the greening bracken;
There they marched
In the shackles of convention
Where the city reached its suburbs
Up to claim them.
And there I sat
Free and unseen
On a wild ling tuft
Listening to Synge
And the song of the mountain.

AFTER AFRICA

As long as I can wield the pen
I will not sit behind computer ware.
My bones are older than me now
If that were possible.
At Christmas time we say hello
And greet again for old time's sake.

I saw you first
Wide eyed with wonder,
On Sabena steps
Propeller bound for Africa.

The jungle night
Could hold no fear
For one who heard
The crush of army boots
Through cornfields
And hushed Resistance.

Bilharzia and childbirth,
The clatter of the cooking pots,
The stoves and stones
That kept the sadza hot,
The parasites,
The twisted cords,
That first Christmas of long ago,
The loneliness
That says hello
Each Christ birth.

Sabena's engines
Roll no more.
The shaft of light
That lit a forest floor
Has long been overgrown.
The paint has blistered
On a mission door,
Where someone might remember.

I saw your safe return
To mother house
That was to be your haven,
Where Europe now united.
You were young again
But tide moved on
Where time wrought havoc
On limb and soul
And mind and bone,
Your lot again to be the helper
Of the helpless,
With that same look
Sabena stole,
But closed doors
Could never dull
Your enthusiasm.

ALLEN AND THE FALCON

"Oh Peregrine! Oh Peregrine!
My cliffs are yours for searching,
My severed crags will guard unseen
Your brood and you when resting;
My creviced face, your hiding place,
My heart by man affronted,
My furrowed brow will show you how
The hunter saves the hunted."

"Oh Allen, still alluring Hill
By Corraig, Djouce and Maulin,
You watched the march of hunting men
Fiodh Cullen through Fiodh Almhaine,
You heard the love song Diarmuid made
In murmurs to the river
Where Gráinne's heart was lost one day
To live in love forever."

"Oh Peregrine, I heard your scream!
We're bound by fate together,
Go tell me if the lark is seen
Above the hummocked heather?
Go tell me if the languid crane
Stands knee deep in the tarn,
And tell me if the sighing reeds
Talk to the croziered fern?

Go out beyond the rills of Cush
Where Figile feeds the Barrow,
And tell me if the eskers blush
With marguerite and yarrow.
Go out beyond the cotton fens
Beyond the móin to Croghan,
And tell me if the summer suns
With purple tinge the fraochan."

"I saw the hazel and the birch,
I saw the crimson berries
With crouching whin and rowan ash
Retreat into the Derries.
I saw the rail tracks cross the bog
From Timahoe descending,
I saw the fumes' emetic rage
On nature's breath offending.

I saw no lark by Croghan Hill
I saw no hummocked heather,
I saw the lilies span the pools
With *drownded* leaves of sorrow.
I saw the hare, his poisoned lair
Forsaken leave the rushes,
I saw the seabhac's shimmer stare
Into the hungered bushes.

The elk has gone from Lullymore
The wild boar from his island,
The callow's call is heard no more,
The red grouse cry is silent.
The lorried men are in the fen
I heard their engines whining,
Beneath the crown of startled whin
There's fuse and powder mining."

"Oh Conán Maol, *Tá muid i ngéill,*
Your fighting spirit fails us,
The sordid boon of Worthsworth's lay
With other worth assails us.
Mo grá, mo grá, mo peregrine
Our plight we'll pledge together,
That we might cling by rock and wing
In love to save each other."

ASYLUM

I

Her joints ached
A dull twinge
As she reached across
The compost heap
Plucking mushrooms
From the breath of morning.
Hands, wrists, back,
Throbbed like a bogland fire,
Another flare up
That would smoulder on
When the conflagration seemed to cease.
Joints were like that,
Red, hot, erupting, unpredictable.
Then she thought of home,
The cobbled cultures once imposed,
The soldiers and the forests,
The fields
Where she hid
From marauding hordes.
Her back ached,
But she was safe
Resigned
To pick the mushrooms
From a compost heap
For export.

II

I am sick,
Sick in my heart
And here, sick in my head.
Two thousand pigs
In one day
Cut, Cut,
Two thousand pigs,
Four thousand sides.
I am no butcher,
I know computers,
Many programmes,
I am not a stupid man.
I know engines.
This is not the work for me,
Two thousand pigs,
Spines and brains and offal;
Cut, Cut, Cut,
In one day,
But I am far away
And I am sick
Here in my heart
For home.

III

Something for you
From our country,
Taste a little,
Read a little,
Craft work
From our country.
Remember me?
László Papp
Yes?
And Puskás.
László Papp is dead,
Died last year,
But still
Ferenc Puskás,
Our only Magyar,
Our only English!
This is
From our country.

IV

Four days to the holidays,
Four days;
After seven months and one day
I will see my wife
Again.
Then at the traffic lights
I met Stevie Wonder.
Zoom zoom,
The car
Just sped away,
And I am left,
No work,
No pay,
Just pain,
An X-ray
And the sound of Stevie Wonder.
Four days to the holidays
And I will not see
My son,
Because of the traffic lights
And the getaway
Of Stevie Wonder.

V

I left for England
When I was fifteen,
Didn't have a word
Of English then. I was
A Paddy from Connemara!
It was hell at first
The site, the digs,
The workplace;
But then
I paid my way
To Germany.
The bus stopped
In Frankfurt,
I've been there ever since.
Went back to school
When I was twentyfive
To learn to read
And speak the English.
That's how it came to be.
Came home last year
But all is changed,
Changed everywhere,
Foreigners in Connemara.
I could not stay,
Not a quiet corner anywhere,
To sit and sip a beer,
And now I'm here,
A stranger in Ireland.

VI

Vilnius is my city.
I was born there,
Here, in this picture
On the sokoladas bar
I brought for you...
I was a student there.
Here, I work in the chill rooms
And the sluice,
Cleaning here, cleaning there,
From hot to cold,
Hot to cold,
Always cold in the chill room,
And the sluice.
But Vilnius
Is my home.
I was accountant there.
Vilnius
Is my city.

VII

A Big Thanks God
I'm better now.
At work, little English.
Now Lithuanian, and Latvian,
And Russian.
I want to learn
To speak the English,
But at work
No English
And no Irish.
I now translate
Lithuanian and Latvian
Into Russian
In a mushroom field
In Cairbre.

VIII

I go home to Poland
Next week
I go home.
After two years I'm no good,
The Boss says
I'm no good,
No good to build.
The scaffold fell
And now I am no good.
I must go home
To fix myself,
But that's life,
As you here say
That's life.

HAPPY BIRTHDAY

The Cherries are shedding
Their Blossoms to-day
And weighed down they waited
To send their bouquet.

The swallows are back
To the eves where they grew
And loudly they chatter
Of how the year flew.

The Bluebells are lining
The paths in the wood,
And they watch the years pass
Down the lanes where they stood,

And life threading softly
Through clouds and through cheer
Will say Happy Birthday
In April each year.

BEDROOM PORTRAIT

That young man there!
Who is he?
The officer in the photograph?

My Father!
He was killed at twenty seven
On the front
In the Great War.
He went away in May,
Left my mother expecting.
He said that if he volunteered
There was an officer's job;
There was conscription in those days,
And there he is
In his regalia.
He never came home,
Killed in October,
Bled to death they said
In the days before *penicillin.*
It was hard on my mother then,
She was expecting me,
And I was born
In this house here,
Eighty seven years ago
Beneath that photograph.

Gate on the past

By the Gave

BY THE GAVE

I

Wheelchairs

They brought the wheelchair
As far as here one year;
Condemned to death:
Aren't we all?
He tried to be normal,
But they grouped him
With the others,
The wheelchair dictating
What his category should be.
He used to do the physical,
But now he felt
Like half a man
And did as he was told,
Their common bond,
The wheelchairs.
He could not escape
From some he did not care for,
And dared not say so.
Two more would graduate
To them this year,
Another two were gone.

The hill did not seem so steep
Before.

II

One step more

He was six foot four
And fourteen stone,
A giant of the second row.
We watched him jump
And run
And sometimes score,
Before the accident.
His father watched him now,
Admiration still
Heaving in his chest
As he saw him strive
To balance on his tripod.
A second time
He learned to walk,
More painful than the first.

Determination had reward
With one step more.

III

Communicating

Alone, all alone,
Another painful outburst
The only expression.
Hormones surged
Disruptive as ours,
Muscles cramped,
Clamped, vice-like,
And the articulation
Of eyes pleading communication.
The pathway thronged,
Aloneness
With togetherness.
Music from below
Breaks from its moorings,
Wafting upwards,
To be lost
Somewhere on its everlasting way
Beyond the stratosphere.

CEILÍ HOUSE REMEMBERED

The Christmas trees are gathered
The bonfire's leaping high,
Orion at its rising
Has climbed the Eastern sky;
At the crossroads of Baltrasna
As the New Year's ushered in
Strike music for the dancing,
Let Ceilí House begin.

Bring out the Reels, the Hornpipes,
The rosin on the strings,
The roads to retrospection
That Ceilí House will bring;
O'Murchú was foremost,
O'Dubhghail, Peter Browne,
Then Hanrahan's "Hello There"
To greet the music throng.

There were Lutes and Flutes and Harpists
Tin Whistles' twirling notes
At MacGabhann's house in Ashbourne
There were Bodhráns made from goats,
And twenty seven fiddleplayers
Lined up in a row
Played "The cow that ate the blanket"
When Tony raised the bow.

We remember Josie Murphy
In *The Claremen*'s where we met
Where the Murphys faced McMahons
For the makings of a set,
The Hillarys, the Brodies,
Aiden Vaughan, Paddy King,
"Colonel Frazier","Toss the Feathers",
"Lucy Campbell" with the Keanes.

There were two from Miltown Malbay
Tried to show us fancy steps
When Mick McGuane forninst them
Made the floor quake with his leaps,
And for those who hesitated
When dancing on the spot…
When Josie shouted, "House Around!"
We "Housed round" like a shot!

We had Donlons there from Longford,
O'Learys, MacAoghain,
The Havertys from Galway
And from Cork, O'Muineacháin,
Mick O'Connor from The Castle
Michael Tubridy was there
When the music man from Cavan
Met the dancing girl from Clare.

Oh Europe, do not smother us
Or take our soul away,
Allow us to enrich you
Where the Concertinas play;
On the shrine that was the hearthstone
'Ere Riverdance began
Let the dancers dance the dances
Till the Reels come round again.

CHRISTMAS SPONSOR

I am a little goat
Loose in Malawi,
The Tsetse fly brewing
A storm in my head,
I once chewed the flowers
And the shrubs in the garden,
But then I was sponsored
And sent here instead.

I am a young heifer
By the banks of The Sabi
Where the elephant grasses
And bamboos are high.
I am watching a crocodile
Snooze by the river,
But although he is sleeping
He's opened one eye!

I'm a Rhode Island Red
That crows to the morning,
Where The White Nile from its mountain
Embraces The Blue,
With my neck stretched for cheering
I noticed a warning,
There's someone there watching
My neck stretching too.

I'm an organic turkey
Free range in the stubbles,
High stepping through fields
Where the corn once grew.
With my gobbledegook,
My snood and my wattle,
I thrived on the gleanings
Of what I was due.
But it's now nearing Christmas
I've changed my ambitions,
*Will somebody **please***
*Send **me** on the Missions.*

COLOURS OF EMOTIONS

The bed,
The chair,
The empty room,
The mirror
Colourless in Arles;
I have news for you today, Vincent
Your room was thronged in d'Orsay,
The biggest crowd at the station.

I looked across the forty years,
To that battleground of the emotions;
We lead,
Encourage,
Sometimes show the way,
Oppose the stray,
But we are human too
And realise the loss.

The Gleaners bend
And pick, and bind,
Primary colours in the setting sun;
Idyll and reality.
The bell tolls by Millet's spire;
A grandmother's respect
Saluting the Angelus;
Idyll and reality.

A wind chilled the isobars
By Saggart's granite steeple,
Idyll and reality;
Ah, Eamonn, Eamonn
Did *you* not see in you
The beauty that the whole world
Saw in you?

Higher Line
Lower Line,
Meissonier's lines of loyalty;
Dignity in adversity,
Bonaparte in his wilderness.

Again the bell
Tolling its reality;
Jesus, remember me,
A Gregorian drone
Reluctant to let go,
In unified emotions
Of a child remembered -
When you come into your kingdom.

The door closed
On an empty room
Where the biggest crowd had gathered
And one could not grow old.

DEATH OF A CYCLIST

Marco Pantani is dead,
Found alone,
In a hotel room
In Rimini.
The Pirate fled the Pyrenees,
An Eagle lost his Alpine day.

Who killed Pantani?
Was it I
With my remote control,
Willing you on
And ever onwards,
In a sitting room,
On the Alpe d'Huez
Where others failed,
Or clinging with you
To your fragile steed
As you fled fearless
Down the Galibier?

Or *was it you* that killed Pantani
With your bandanas and your logos,
Your colours draped on hoardings
Hungry for a moving screen
That stole minutes with your Pirate,
Dancing pedals on Ventoux,
That dead volcano
Where nothing grows?

Or *was it you*
Son of Hippocrates,
With your pestle and your mortar
Grinding recipes and potions,
Prescriptions for aggression
That propelled you through those searing peaks
And sped you
Down below?

Or *could it be yourself,*
With ambition fraught
Till success became addiction
And to win became the drug
Your mind
Could not control?

I thought of you today
On a fog and frost December,
With the tempo getting smarter
On a slope I hadn't noticed there before,
And as the echelon was gaining
With their cackle getting sharper
Like wild geese in their phalynx,
I thought of you
As they escaped
Along an esker that was waiting
And I heard their cackle fading
Into receding fog.

This is how it must have been
When all the labs were done,
When other new pretenders
Precocious on the hillside
Attacked, where you had won,
Where you revelled in escaping,
Till the glycogen was gone.

Is there more to life, I thought, than clamour
And reflected adulation,
And as I pedalled homewards
Thought of you who would not know
An autumn rising
Or a ripening sun,
Colours faded,
Glamour jaded,
Mistral gone.
I thought of you
In a hotel room,
Alone,
While the world,
Its colours blazing,
Just moved on.

EASTER

I talked to a man
Who had nothing to do;
He went home to bed
Because it was Good Friday.
His usual hostelry was shut.
Did this not demonstrate
The spiritual nature
Of how much more man is
Than axons and synapses
And computer particles?

I saw a man
Whose hand shook
As he firmly clenched the flame
On Holy Saturday night.
"Do you renounce the Devil?"
"To Hell with him" he thought,
"And all his pomps and promises".
I was deprived through fear
Of so much I could have known,
But it doesn't matter now.

I watched a man
Who stopped for breath
On Easter Sunday morning.
He leaned across a farmyard gate
To watch a lamb
Wriggle in excitement, from nose to tail
And dunt the udder,
Where the first bluebell
Lifted its head in hopeful resurrection
From the back of some forgotten ditch.

EXCHANGES

I

Bruised Apples

What can I do?
I am on the shady side of the hill.
It takes a lot
To get to where the sun is.
The bruised apples
Are littered all around,
Beginning their decay.
The bright red ones
Are high up there,
Out of reach,
Promising encouragement.

I wrote a letter to myself
When I was low...
I spelled out all my fears.
I will wait
And answer them myself
When I am calm.
I did a spring-cleaning
Of my mind,
I cleared the clogged up
Wardrobes of my worries.
The pen is a great friend,
"Mightier than the Sword," they say.
It is mightier than prescriptions.
I pen my own conclusions
Looking all around
At bruised apples
On the ground.

II

Bad News

"I was at the hospital the other day"
"I know"

"The surgeon said I had a tumour"
"I know"

"They sent me for a C and T scan
I think they call it,
But the results have not come back yet"
"They came back this morning"

"Is that why you called out?"
"It is"

"Well, is it good news or bad?"
"Not good"

"Will there be an operation?"
"There will be, of some sort"

"And if they can't remove it,
What next?"
"There will be chemotherapy"

"Some of them are tricky enough to get at"
*"If you want to go to Dublin
The surgeon doesn't mind"*

"I wouldn't know about these things.

Which would be the best?
I'll leave that up to you"
"One would be handy for visiting,
The other would have more facilities.
It would be better for the follow-up."

"I suppose we should go for the best"
"I think we should
The surgeon is making a special appointment
To see you"

"I'll go anyway,
These things have to be faced."

"It's a sentence
Isn't it?"

"It is"

III

November

On the dark days
Everything is down around you.
If I hear of disease at all
That's me!
In my heart I know I'm healthy
But my head overrules it all.
If it gets in there
It lodges in the brain and will not go.
At night I say I'm sorry
But throughout the day I cannot cope.
There's just the four walls
And November.
I could have a great life
But I cannot,
The days close in
In November.

IV

The Attack

"They're important people
At the head of things", they say,
"But life is short
And we should get through it
As best we can.
It was terrible
The amount of death
And destruction
In just a few hours.
They're terrible unruly people,
Haeverals some of them,
And haeverals on the other side too.
What do they want
Or what is there to gain?"

A moose was excavated
From the ice,
A dinosaur from his layer of dust;
An imprint
On the Pleistocene.

V

The Spirit Crowd

I went to see the spirit crowd
As I call them.
They were all on their knees
Going Yum, Yum, Yum.
I went down
On my knees too
And went Yum Yum Yum,
Along with them.
There's a spiritual side
To most of us,
But it shouldn't take over
Entirely.

VI

Because I Went Away

Because I left
They thought I should not grieve,
But I am grieving too,
Both for the loss
And for what there might have been.
There was not a day
I did not pray,
But maybe someday too
They might understand.
I tried, and tried,
God knows I tried,
But there was no other way,
And now I am not allowed to grieve
Because I went away.
I only think
Of what there might have been,
And hope some day
That they will understand
How every dream
Cannot be answered.

VII

No one would believe me

A little bit of my past
Crept up on me today.
I cannot cry.
I cannot talk about it.
It is there all the time.
Am I the only one
That gets the torment,
Or do they think
That I am able?.
I wrote it in a letter
What I thought,
And burned it,
And still it will not go away.
I might tell when he dies!
Different times
And different people.
All the time now
I drift in and out of depression,
The good days passing.
No one would believe me.
He was adored,
Adored,
No one would believe me.

VIII

Nightcalls

He called me
Several times in the night.
He's more contented
And sleeps a lot
By day.
He worries about many things;
The mare due in the lower field.
He called me in the dark
To look at her.
His blood has dropped again.
If anything should happen
I'll let you know.

Outside
A girl stopped
To pluck wild roses
On a lane leading to nowhere.

IX

Euphoria

She finished the treatment today.
There was great euphoria
In our house,
The treatment over.
She could have got one more
But that was all for now.
There could be new treatments
But the marrow tests were low.
She had a good day
And might be home tomorrow.
There was great euphoria in our house.

X

Silences

She had a long history of silences,
Of bruises, excuses,
Of verbal assaults
That left no mark
But gnawed away inside the soul.
Now the children
Used the same names,
Doubly hurtful
Because they did not know their meaning,
And, grown in violence,
Knew no other way.
And when she did find love,
Imperceptibly,
When someone listened,
It must remain
Forever secret,
Lest it might be said
The years of pain
Were vindicated.

XI

Commonplace

We have grown immune to death,
And to killing;
Another gangland murder
Making place names familiar.
We expect to hear it now.
There are so many
That we do not remember.
What once was news
Now is commonplace.
It then belonged to far away,
To make-believe,
To the film world
Where crime was entertainment;
Now,
Why are we surprised
When death is commonplace?

XII

On my own

I am on my own,
You'll have to help me.
I miss him when I come home.
I talk to him
As if he was still here,
And when he asks
Who won?
I say
I didn't anyway.
But there's always next week
And tomorrow.
I feel close to him then,
But I still miss him
Terribly.

XIII

The Inquest

He was at peace today
In his new club vest,
Unaware of the hearts
That were broken.
The coroner was kind.
He did not know,
How could he know
How many hearts
Would stop
In that instant
When he stepped
Outside of time
On impulse.

XIV

On repeating exams

Sometimes on life's pathways,
With their twistings and their turnings,
With their uphills and descents,
With their obstacles which we negotiate,
We learn more,
See more,
And get more satisfaction
Than on
The Interstate Highway.

YOUR ROOM

There are many rooms
Inside my head.
I often visit yours.
There I can stay awhile
And tell you things
That no one else
Would need to know.

I saw a thrush this morning
Outside the windowpane;
He looked so forlorn
Amid the snowdrops.
He came one day before
When you were tired,
Too tired, and did not notice.

A wren came through the open door,
When we spoke of you today;
Or was it open?
He flitted through
Half frightened places
Until he found his way home.

They were all in tune
And missing you.
I'll come back into your room
Again today,
There's so much more
I need to say.

FLASHBACK

When will the f***ing stop
When will the f***ing stop
The f***ing has to stop
And the bleeding.
The Bastard
Will not make me cry,
Will not make me cry.
Dignum et justum est.
Sursum corde
Habemus ad dominum.
The Bastard
Will not make me cry.

The incense
The surplice;
Twisted lace
On twisted vines,
Embroidered grapes
That crucified,
Only those at the abyss
Will understand
The flashback,
The soul pain
The mind pain
That does not go away
But burns ingrained
With acrid bitterness.

Dignum et justum est.
The Bastard.
Charcoal chains
On twisted minds,
Thurifer
To neutralise
With fragrance
The sweat, the fear,
The exocrine.
Sanctus, Sanctus, Sanctus.
The Bastard
Will not make me cry.

Bitter tears
Will dissipate
On cheeks
Burrowed useless,

Or are they useless?
Each crisis
A step
Forward for renewal

Resolution
Must start from here,
Start from here.
De profundus clamavi ad te...
Out of the depths I cry...

After rain
The morning can be brighter.

FLIGHTPATHS

In the flightpath of the airways,
In the shadow of the deep,
I can hear him whisper softly
It's no problem where I sleep.
He will watch the flights departing
Each September overhead,
He will hear them safe returning
When the parting prayers are said.

He walked among the needful
His head above the throng,
He stooped to help the feeble,
He made the poor belong;
Where the rock stands by the fountain
And the quiet tears are shed
We can hear the words *No problem*
When the parting prayers are said.

When the year turns in September
And the leaves begin to sway
With the chestnuts by the river
Softly falling where they lay,
We can hear the voice recalling
As the parting prayers are said
And the bells across the river
Tolled *No problem* overhead.

The 5ᵗʰ station

Pol an Eas, Glendalough

GLENDALOUGH

I came back again today
To where the crags weep
Moss tears of the mountains
To the lakes below.
I climbed the goat trail path
To where a peace would grow
Into the pool
Beyond the waterfall.
You would have known
That pre-Gregorian drone,
That ice age polishing
Of an unrelenting stone.
You froze in anger
When Art O'Neill was lost,
On the perishing Féar Gorthas
Beyond the saving reach of Glenmalure.

Along the wooded path
I watched them trail today
With map and book and snapshot
In Gallic and Germanic droves.
They passed the gangling oaks
By your monastic door
As once they fled
The Goth and Visigoth,
The Hun and heathen hordes.
Today they seek for peace,
The peace that Mammon does not know,
In your retreat,
In their retreat into the whinlight
And the gospels
By the shore.

HISTORY

There is evil
In every century
And every season of the world;
When we talk of wars
Of ancient Greece and Rome
Of Medes or Persians,
Of battles won and subjugations,
Every trireme had its slaves,
Every boat its chains,
Every army had its young men
Choked in fear,
Bowels loose in trepidation.
Behind the marching vans
Of Xerxes and of Cyrus
And of Xenaphon.
They bled and died,
Wounds festered
In the name of progress;
Power sanitised by time,
Thucydides with papyrus reeds
Told young men's dreams
And hopes like ours
That were strangled
On the pages.
But that was outside time,
They were outside time -
In history

LA CORUNA

I was thinking football,
You were thinking poems;
Deportivo La Coruna
And you mentioned Sir John Moore.

I walked against the hillside
Met the pilgrims coming home,
"Buenos Dies," cockles, rucksacks,
And they buried Sir John Moore.

They streamed across the cobbles,
Chirping words I do not know,
Took a rest on Monte do Gozo,
Sang their songs before they go.

"We have not been travelling too much
Only five days on the road",
Snowless ski-sticks through the wattles
And a light heart is no load.

Way down on the Camino
They're still struggling on below,
Trudging through the Middle Ages,
Pilgrims on their journey home

LIFE'S EBBING

"God blast you to hell, Nurse,
Nurse, Where are you?"
The repetitious crake
Of mind extinguishing.
"Damn your soul to hell, Nurse,
Nurse, Where are you?"

The answer came in gentler crake,
Another soul
Disintegrating.
"Sacred Heart of Jesus, help me,
Sacred Heart of Jesus,
Help me"

Onward, onward flowed the tide
That swept away
Small farmsteads,
Dwelling homes
That now were pensions
Brochured for the market.

Nest eggs
Became life's flotsam
That disappeared into the gullyholes
Where new fortunes grew
And other mansions rose
In the ebbing of civility.

MORECAMBE BAY

Coffee and Jaffa Cakes;
The rain on the conservatory
Was musical.
The tide ebbed and flowed
Amid the cockle shells.
We browsed the shops
And the newspapers.
The tide rose again
Amid the cockle pickers;
Then all was silent
By Morecambe Bay.

23 Chinese cockle pickers drowned
at Morecambe Bay, 5th February, 2004.

OLDER THAN THE CENTURY

For days we watched
The ebb tide of his breath
And heard its fretful flow,
The shuffling
That his hands made
With the clothes.
"I'm tidying up," he said, "I'm ready"
And yet, he took us by surprise
When it was time to go.
A chestnut fell,
Its tegument split open
On an autumn floor,
An apple
Clinging with an orchard leaf
Let go.

He was older
Than the century
But never understood
How anyone
Who had enough
Could look for more.
Contentment was his lot
And work was never hard, he said
When there was enjoyment there.
There are some who write,
And some whose lives are books
That should be penned,
So we can take a leaf
To guide us
To the end.

Autumn Leaves

An Island Road

ON WINDERMERE

The foxglove starved purple
On a rock crevice,
Light against Silurian grey.
War planes from Lancashire
Scarify the silence,
Hawk Hunters
Built to kill.

The boats on Windermere
Ply up and down
Creating waves
That gently dissipate
Beneath a lone cygnet
With a watching parent
Bobbing timeless
On an ice age pond.

PATTERNS

It must be Thursday;
He's sidling home
Half tanked,
The Social Welfare spent.
He will be back tomorrow
First thing,
Square box secure
On his carrier
For the supermarket's cheap grog,
Hair of the dog, you know
To take him through the day
Till evening beckons.

The footpath moved once
As he went home.
Leaning on his handlebars
He felt the soft cement
Underfoot.
In yielding steps
The arc of bicycle tyres
Was imprisoned Hollywood-like
Indelibly
On a setting footpath,
A routine recurring,
Where only footprints remain.

REMEMBERING

There are memories
That only the mind can capture,
There are scenes
That no lens should recall;
Glimpses of the spirit world
Where soul meets soul
And it is profane to record.

I went back today
When all was quiet
And the throb and throng of mourners
Had dissipated,
Where flowers hung limp
With petalled memories clinging to a stem
As the outside world returned.

I watched a plane cross
The granite in the green,
Tracing Ogham lines on the firmament,
Its sound an after-thought
Of the wind
Through the cross-crowned stones,
Where someone sat remembering.

RETIREMENT

It's a terrible change
After forty years
Of getting up
When the first frost
Has trapped the dew.
No one knows what it's like.
I see a man beside me
Couldn't wait to get out,
And now he's like
A tiger in a cage.
There are days
When no one calls
And we wait for someone,
Anyone, to bring the news.
It's a terrible change
When the mat is pulled,
And you return unprepared
To where you started,
To an echo-chamber
Where once you laughed
With children.

SÍLE

There are times when we see real beauty
In this life;
The crisp of the frost on the early morning,
Jupiter threading its way through the twins
On a February night,
Fading into the brighter light of the half moon;
A life that is more perfect
Than we ever thought possible,
Perfect, because of its goodness,
Perfect, because of its innocence;
The innocence that says,
"I love my food and
I love myself"
And you come to admire that innocence
And that honesty;
A life that says, "I am,"
When your greeting is,
"You're looking well,"
And stopping short, you know
That's right!
And it was a privilege
To be touched by that innocence
And that goodness.

We will remember the innocence;
We will remember the goodness;
We will remember the singing.

Slán leat, Síle,
Slán.

Lourdes in February

ST. CRONAN'S ABBEY

I walked through Time's archway
Where the Moneen
Bathes the chestnuts
That bloom by the Bell Tower.

Some see here the gateway
To the liberation
And contemplation
Of the soul.

Some see the gaol
Where outside
The river escapes
In its cascade to meet the Brosna.

The Franciscans heard
That same cascade
Before Cronan's day,
Serenading history.

Who are remembered?
Those who passed through the door
To the whisper
Of evening vespers?

Or those who passed out again
To be assimilated
In the busy world,
With its success and its forgetfulness?

STRESS

When I want to know
What stress is,
I listen to
The wind in the chimney.
The wind in the chimney whispers.

I am alone
Comfortable,
Listening to the fire,
Crackling,
The purr of the peat
And the branches
Releasing heat
Stored ten thousand years before;
And then I hear
The wind in the chimney
Comforting.

"Sorry!...
I can't do it.
I cannot record that!..." said the cameraman,
"Too much interference,
Too much bloody interference!
Can you not hear
The bloody wind in the chimney?"

SUNDAY MORNING

She moved between the trailing drapes,
Willow tall and full of grace,
Attractive accent clipped,
Continental,
Serving tables, far from home.
Angular toast
Triangular butter pats
Deploying silverware;
"Excuse me!"
"Have you got some Mor-Gur-een..."
The silence shattered,
With irritable vowels
And hardened consonants.
Ambience grated.
We had unseeded prunes for breakfast.

A life size stallion,
The Byerley Turk
With barefoot groom
Looked down on his array
Of morning cereals,
Mangoes, pears
With honeyed melons
And missing "Mor-Gur-een."

The river eased its stately flow
By artificial pools of rainbows,
A mile of prestige bondage
Freed beyond the bridge
Where brown trout breed.
I saw an ancestor today,
A prize
Glass caged and weighed,
A trophy of the spinners.

"The Times Digest"
Essential Sunday morning reading!
Two hundred crossword clues
And more, with graceful foreign smile.
We did all this for others
Before the tide
Raised economic graphs
That washed our innocence away.

I hoped the readings might not be,
Might be
St. Paul today.
Tipperary beef and Woodland mushrooms
Beyond sophistication,
Beyond the reach of calling bell,
Beyond the champagne toast
Proposed with tinkling cymbals.
You were not advertised today
Paul or Saul of Tarsus
Or Luke physician of the mountain.

The great proud stallion,
Charger of The Boyne,
Fecund sire of the Male-tail line,
Captive Turk,
Equine progenitor,
Your litany framed
By our breakfast cereal,
The river stealing towards oblivion,
A segment caught between hill and sea,
The brown trout cased
By angler's rod and gillie's basket;
All captive here.
We escaped in,
Will escape out
With equal felicity and satisfaction.

A primula beneath the portico
Blushed bashful where it chanced to see the light.

I did not want you standing there, you know
In that pampered room of artifice,
Of His and Hers
Of crested wear
Of lavender and private safe
Where rust and moth might not consume
And thieves not enter.
I did not want you there
For when I thought of you
Where mind met mind
And soul met soul
I saw you reach for beauty
Way beyond the stars.

THANK GOD FOR CHRISTMAS

Thank God for Christmas
Where the year's loose ends are tied
And tidied,
And we are free to say
What other months and feasts and days
Forbid with their conventions;
Where we look deeper still
To where important ones are sought
And brought from year's obscurity;
Where respects are paid
And maybe some allowed
Before the lengthening days usurp
The fledgling year,
That, growing stronger with the sun,
Takes us on to pathways
Of uncertain charting
Till we draw breath again
And pause
At cycle's turning,
To witness rebirth
And appreciate again with you
What's true.

THE BOCCE PLAYER

(OR, A DAY IN JUNE)

Who knows what the game of Bocce is?
Who has seen the Bocce Player smile?
I wrote to the Health Board
For the man who wrote to Santa Claus
When he was twenty-one
For I had seen the Bocce Player smile.

The rugby men stood round the tunnel's mouth
Applause heaped on the vanquished,
Pulverised before in ruck and maul,
More ruthless than Baghdad's fall
The day the Bocce player smiled.

A giant from Ukraine
Fought for the world crown.
His hands upset the throne,
The champion stumbled round.
The moneyed men
His laurel wreath denied,
And sent him to obscurity
The day the Bocce player smiled.

They laughed at Ascot
When the streaker strode,
In bowler hat
And dickie-bowed,
But that's another smile.

The poppies reached their heads
Above the wheat
To greet the sun;
I saw the crimson in their cups
Because the wheat was not mine.

The marguerites danced
On sandbanks for today
With no thought beyond tomorrow,
The envy too of Solomon,
And I thanked my God
That I was given shoes
That I could wear...

And I wrote for the man
Who wrote to Santa Claus
When he was twenty one,
Because there are so many days
Like this
In every year,
And the Bocce Player smiled.

THE BODHRÁN PLAYER

The Bodhrán is silent
The sunlight is shade,
The last note on the goatskin
To the reel has been played.

He burst on the catwalk,
Our hearts to engage,
He linked us in laughter,
The world his stage.

How can we stay silent?
How could we regret
The laugh without blemish
He bestows on us yet?

THE BOTANIC GARDENS

Taxus and Thuja,
The Great Sequoia
Reached its red arms upwards.
By its girth
A sapling girl
Beamed love texts to the airwaves.
Behind a glass,
Mute motionless
Two lovers sat.
He moved
To guide her drinking cup.
Her lips were parted
With words garbled,
Right hemisphere immobile.
Then he rose
And gently backwards
Eased her wheelchair
Through a yielding door.
"I can do it," "Thanks," he said,
And raised a shield
Against the raindrops.
A young girl beamed beneath the Great Sequoia
And the sign that read
"Rose Garden"
Where an autumn bloom
Was fading.

THE CARPENTER

"Ambition's made of sterner stuff," he roared,
And struck the board with hammer's cleaving blow,
He split the timber rings of summers' growth
And brought the nave ascending from below.
He called out for the auger and the plane
And saw the wood curls tumbling on the floor,
He saw, in thought, the child who learned to play
But gimlet pierced the cross the nails would bore.

"The poor that cried when Caesar wept," he chose,
Among the Shona huts he made his home;
He railed with Stratford bard and bible quote
As beam with beamed support the chancel rose.
There is a silence where the hammer fell;
That silence recollects a mission bell.

THE ENFIELD ROAD

For years I've heard proclaiming,
About the Enfield Road,
And how its twists and turnabouts
Our peace of mind erodes,
So take the road from Dublin,
To the Enfield roundabout,
And leave for Edenderry,
Where the arrows point you south.

The first conundrum meets you
As you top the turnpike ridge,
It's an end-wall on the river
As you slow for Johnstownbridge,
Where the lorries jolt their engines
And their drivers start to boil,
As the walkers run for cover
And the bikes go single file.

Then out beyond the river
Watch out for vertigo,
For the roadway starts to wriggle
As it goes through Kilshanroe.
And the cats' eyes have gone crosseyed,
From reflecting beams of light,
That wave one way, then the other
As the cars wind through the night.

Then right at Boylan's mansion,
Sitting stately on its hill,
The road turns into S-hooks
Like the S-hoops round Ardkill,
And the cattle watched a hedgehog,
As he tried to cross the track,
Grow befuddled in the middle,
With the white lines coming back.

Next up the hill to Drehid,
You straighten at The Sweep,
Where the fields are full of Herefords,
And Potterton's full of sheep.
There's not a Red Cow roundabout,
With stoplights or with yields,
But there's lots of hemi-roundabouts,
To go round and round the fields.

Then, T-square right for Carbury
Left T-square, Grogan's, please,
Right T-square now at Newbury,
You'll get there by degrees.
With The Boyne left right behind you
In its Trinity abode,
You're straight for Edenderry
On a very crooked road.

A politician heading homewards,
Heliclopping through the air,
Saw the ribbon road beneath him,
Through the fields of North Kildare.
Thought this track is worth preserving,
Like the Trail to Sante Fe,
Or the mountain paths of Oregon,
From the Great Wyoming Trail.

He saw another roadway ripple,
Through Clonkeen by Cole's demesne,
Said "Don't touch that strip of asphalt,
It's the county's last chicane."
And, being a wise one at the hustings,
Thought, "election time's in doubt,
If we fix that road from Enfield
We'll have nought to shout about."

So, Here's to The Road from Enfield,
A most contentious prize!
A monument to straight lines,
And to every crow that flies.
That makes a ten mile journey
To twelve or more extend
With inflation round each corner
As we go round the bend.

THE MOORING

I went to a funeral
The other day of someone
I onetime knew, a doctor friend

Who lived his life the far side
Of the fen. He was such fun,
They said, a man who could not

Say no. I watched the old men
Line the aisle and nod and smile
And shake the hands as they said so.

They never spoke his name without
His daughter's too, and what befell
So long ago. He knew he was

Not well, and when at time to go
The boat he loved was moored and primed
Where every rising sun would find

And bring to life the Teddy Bear
That once at night a child
Would not let go.

THE REAR WINDOW

A beam of light fell
Newgrange-like across
The window frame, the sash,
The lace, the architrave.
It crept wingless
Through the tubes and chains
Bringing with it resurrection.
I was free, free in my sarcophagus,
My mind free to journey out
Beyond the trees that robed each spring,
Free to tumble with the swallows
Full of the delights of Africa,
Free to career in careless flight
Where starlings float like stringless kites
Above their restful branches.
I am not bound down;
My mind is free to dream
And courage streams
Through this rear window
To make me *be* my dreams.

THINKING OF KAVANAGH

I often think of Patrick Kavanagh
In weather like this,
Leaning over the wide mouth
Of a wooden barrel,
Where the potatoes were waiting
In rotation
For the spraying.
There was no blight warning yet
But it was everywhere
Hanging about in the humidity.
I was in Paris last week.
I went on the Eiffel tower
Almost all the way
To the top.
Indescribable is the only word
I could use to describe it.
Looking down
At the crook of the river
I was thinking about the changing face
Of Europe
And of the world,
And of Clonmullen,
Where there were potatoes once
That needed spraying.

THOUGHT PEBBLES

Thought pebbles tossing
On the brain waves of time,
Ebbing and re-ebbing
To refine and redefine,
Beachcombers searching
Words along the tide,
Listening to the rhythms
Eliding and collide.

Out in the deep bay
Oysters ever turn
Irritating, agitating,
Laminating pearl.
Scruple is the sandstone,
Scruple is the grain,
Scruple is the thought-stone
Polishing the pain.

Jailboats are sailing,
Paintings on the wave,
Fishermen are claiming
Prisoners in a cave.
Some see a thought grow
Till the pearl gain,
Some see the gemstone,
Some see the chain.

TOLERANCE

We are the proportions of things,
Ratios of each absolute;

Not all computer
For we can see the hope
The snowdrop brings,

Not all dreamer,
For we can taste the juice
Of Eden's ripened bough,

Not all appetite,
For we can anticipate
A joy deferred,

Not all sacrament,
For we can know the plan
That protects each part,

And saves us from intolerance.

WHITE ROSES AND RED

There were white roses there, and red
Chrysanthemums with laurel leaf
That spoke of love and loyalty;
More fierce than words could ever speak.

They brought a photograph of you,
Of teenage dreams in black and white,
To offer an unwavered view,
A *slí na fírinne* of life.

The dancing shoes that often thrilled
And trebled through each changing reel
Were tendered to a parting tune,
But now *The Blackbird's* beat is stilled.

The candle of your faith was laid
Among the symbols of your name,
It travelled through a globe in change
With lighted flame that never dimmed.

And next they brought your life's award
For *rising step* and *square quadrille*,
For one who could the world enthrall
Would seek to teach the lowly still.

The last they brought that you might hold,
The *geansaí* that your kith had known,
And in the billows that enfold
We watched the colours match the rose.

TRUST

Once,
You were
In the realms of hope
And possibility,
Hope,
Without possibility;

Imperceptibly
Hope became its possibility
With reassurances
And trust,

Enough
To last
A lifetime.

Bluebell path

An Island Road

A mountain stream

TWO STREAMS

I

I want to go back again to the river
Where the waves struggle
To become one another,
And the mountain trout leap
In the half light
To disappear in the splash
Before words can say
What the mind already captured,
And the bats, sure in their blindness,
Ply patterns by the rockbridge eye
As the waves disappear
Into sonar shrieks
And the starlight
Of the Earth's revolving.

I want to go back up the mountain,
To where the stream is unsure
Near its source,
Where it fumbles
And funnels through boulders
To find the deeper pools,
To rest awhile
With other streams
That will become one,
And some day
One again
With the sea.

II

Oh! Leave me out here on the mountain
Where the deer step is sure on the slope,
Where the fox in the nightfall is prowling
Alone on the grouse hungry moor.
I can see far below in its yearning,
The boulders dictating its course,
The stream turn away from its wildness
To go back to the town and the smoke,

And below, where the deer leaves the mountain
Runs a stream that one day was close,
Carried off on the contours around it
To be lost to a once kindred source.
And somewhere in its twists and its turning
Where the sea heaves its might on the stones,
Two streams that were lost on the mountain
Find the peace that the sea gives the shore.

UMTALI

I saw your name again today
Inside the back page, sonnet sized
Seal of your achievements.

You spoke in Shona to the morning,
And in the noonday sun
Made clearings of acacia scrub
That you might plant a vineyard.

At night, you watched how heaven's floor
With patines of bright gold
Would light Lorenzo's lines
With thoughts of love for Jessica,
And talked of Marvell, Donne and Crashaw too,
Until you raised a paten of your own
To speak in love
Of different kinds.

Down the path of pioneers you came
Across the Christmas Pass
To Christmas loneliness,
An exile in Mashonaland,
You felt the tug of different worlds,
Umtali to Mutare,
Rhodesia to Zimbabwe,
Matabele in Manikaland.

The red road ribboned down
The mountains of Inyanga,
A cloud of Peugeot dust by day
Descending the escarpment,
To the litany,
Through the placenames,
World's View,
Where a Secretary Bird
Quills trailing
Strutted
In the long grass clearings
Above Troutbeck,
Gate of Heaven, Morning Star,
Help of the Sick,
Regina Coeli
Back to The Gairezi,
With its mission school, its spire,
Its maternity and amoeba beds.

From the west veranda
You watched the setting sun, sink
Beyond the solitary date palm
Opportunist,
Sprung from elephant dung
Of one stray bull
Migrating home
To Portuguese East Africa;
And you talked about the mustard seed
In parables, on Sunday
For those who comprehended.

You stood against excess
And tweaked the World Service,
To the crake of night
And quake of cricket song,
That you might hear your name
Expressed
In struggles
With apartheid.

The Champion of the underdog,
You watched the pack grow restless,
And your dreams outflank
Where whelps matured,
More vicious than before,

And twice exiled,
Of home and then adoption,
On a corridor of beeswax
The steps grew slow
And sank in carpets soft
As mists above The Vumba,
Until the mitre moved no more.

WRITING WORKSHOP

I am a recalcitrant!
I should not be here!
Three nouns, three more nouns,
And an adjective...
Tell me,
Would an artist take the colours
From his palette
And splash the paint,
Later to admire the forms that emerge,
Or would he first conceive
An idea
That colour might bring to fruition?

The Professor left.
The American of the profuse nouns left,
Thank God before the adjectives.
I stayed,
An anarchist,
A seething anarchist,
A curmudgeon.

These were superb people
Led by words
That might produce a pattern.
The South African had an idea,
Thoughts against a background.
Why did *I* not do that?
It sounded impressive
But then, he was a professor too.

Graffiti,
Literate graffiti
Scribbled on a workshop floor.
How would this translate
Into a poem?
Thought transcends the language,
The guttural expression of the word
And would survive perhaps,
But scattered words,
Confetti
On the way.

Poems come from emotions,
From thoughts and painful process
Employing words,
Weighed out for size and shape
And sound and rhythm,
Like an artist at his palette
Contemplating colours of the mind
Or a musician
Picking notes to serve his melody.

I was an outsider again,
Looking at sincere people
Playing word games,
Cheerfully reaching out,
Enjoying their achievements.

The shy person of just one poem,
Of what momentous import
We will never know ...
A secret grief
An unrequited love,
Mistaken maybe,
Too sacred,
Too secret,
Beyond that inner sanctum
That we were not to trespass.
What did she expect?
To have her prayer complete?
It could be her refrain forever,
But she was scared
And we will never know.

The Concertina man
Was honest as his music
With music in his honesty.
The Nordic man
Prolific in three tongues,
Read out his thoughts in one
That we could understand
Then lapsed into another
That rolled out in music from its origin.
The lilt of the Highlands
Selkirk to the Islands,
The Scotsman got the idea too late
That Alexander had not got at all.

I can comment from the outside
And not from within.
Curmudgeon!
There's a noun
And cantankerous is an adjective.
Recalcitrant, recalcitrant,
I know, I know.
I'll do a paper on recalcitrance,
A poster for Vienna
Or Amsterdam or Athens.
I'll be back
A recalcitrant
Within the establishment.

NOTES

ALLEN AND THE FALCON.

Corraig, Djouce, Maulin *…Mountains in Wicklow.*
Móin *…turf or bog.*
Fraochan *…wild bilberry.*
Seabhac *…hawk.*
Tá muid i ngéill *…we are in submission.*

ASYLUM.

Laszlo Papp *…multiple Olympic gold medal winner. He remained amateur due to the political constraints then in place.*
Ferenc Puskas *...Hungary's greatest footballer, later played with Real Madrid.*

COLOURS OF EMOTION.

d'Orsay *…In the d'Orsay Museum the only item without colour in Van Gogh's bedroom is the mirror, which gives life's reflection.*
Millet's spire *…The Angelus and The Gleaners at the Museum.*
Meissonier *…Napoleon returning from battle.*

DEATH OF A CYCLIST.

Alpe d'Huez, Galibiere *…mountain climbs in the Alps on the Tour de France.*
Ventoux *…The mountain where Tom Simpson died.*

FLASHBACK.

Dignum et justum est....it is right and just.
Sursum corde ...lift up your heart.
Habemus ad dominum ...we have raised them up to the
Lord.
The Latin responses of the Mass with their irony of
absent insight.
Sanctus, sanctus, sanctus ...holy, holy, holy.
De profundus clamavi ad te ... Out of the depths I have
cried to you, oh Lord.
Ps. 129 vi (Ps. 130 authorised version)

GLENDALOUGH.

Féar Gortas ...*Faragutha Mountains or "hungry grass"*
where people were lost, and was the ill fated route of
Hugh Roe O'Donnell and Art O'Neill in their escape
from Dublin Castle in 1591.

SUNDAY MORNING.

Byerley Turk ...*The Byerley Turk together with The*
Darley Arabian and The Godolphin Barb are reputed to
be the progenitors of every racing thoroughbred in the
world. He was said to have been captured from the Turks
in the campaign of Emperor Leopold in Hungary in 1686
and was later ridden by Colonel Beyerley at The Battle of
the Boyne in 1690. His portrait, by John Wootton hangs
at The K Club.

UMTALI.

Gairezi.... *a river forming the border between Zimbabwe*
and Mozambique